LAURENCE KING

Published in 2020 by
Laurence King Publishing Ltd
361–373 City Road, London,
EC1V 1LR, United Kingdom
T +44 (0)20 7841 6900
enquiries@laurenceking.com
www.laurenceking.com

This book was produced by
Laurence King Publishing Ltd, London

A catalogue record for this book is available
from the British Library

Senior editor: Andrew Roff
Designer: Florian Michelet

ISBN: 978 1 78627 727 5

Printed in China

Laurence King Publishing is committed to
ethical and sustainable production. We are proud
participants in The Book Chain Project ®
bookchainproject.com

Anna McGovern

Illustrations by Charlotte Ager

Pottering. A Cure for Modern Life

Laurence King Publishing

Contents

Introduction

The definition of pottering is to occupy oneself in a pleasant way but without a definite plan or purpose. 'Pleasant' implies comfort. 'Without a definite plan or purpose' implies freedom.

Often but not always it means spontaneously occupying oneself in small household tasks. This task is not *essential*, but by doing it you might derive the tiniest bit of pleasure. To pick an example, one pottering activity you might try is oiling a hinge. Is the hinge of a door or cupboard squeaking? Make do with what you've got, and dab on some oil with a tissue. Any oil will do – olive or vegetable, even margarine. Swing the door to and fro satisfyingly. Stand back and admire your work.

This book is both a discussion of and a practical guide to pottering. It could be seen as an alternative to ambitious and aspirational books about mindfulness (focusing one's mind in the present moment) and hygge (the Danish idea of comfort and conviviality) – both of which, in their original forms, are splendid concepts, but now, in some cases, have changed out of all recognition. Hygge seems to revolve around acquiring scented candles and faux-fur throws, while a guru-led 'mindful minute' might appear to be a salve for everything, but of course will never be. Where the mind is concerned, a minute isn't enough time to find a solution to anything.

One of the characteristics of pottering is its honesty, its lack of affectation. You could connect meditatively and mindfully to mindless tasks like peeling a potato. You could even go to a potato-peeling workshop. Or practise with the world's finest potatoes. Alternatively, you could just peel any potato, with a potato peeler, at home. When sourcing this potato, look in your cupboard. At the very most, go to the nearest shop.

Pottering is not glamorous. You don't have to put too much effort in, go very far or even do it with others. Pottering is not a lifestyle concept, and it doesn't require practice. Just be.

The consequence of pottering – a feeling of relaxation and contentment – is usually achieved when you make do with what you've got, get moving but don't go too far, don't try too hard and keep it digital-free.

1

Pottering:
the basics

To illustrate the basics of pottering, let's take making a cup of tea as an example.

Fill the kettle with water from the kitchen tap. Dock or plug in your kettle. Switch it on and note the cheeriness of the 'on' light. Wait for the kettle to boil, noticing the first wisps of steam. Listen to the rumble of the kettle change in tone, wait for the bimetallic strip to do its work and hear the click that signals the water is ready.

Pick out a teabag and pop it in a mug. It could be your favourite mug but it doesn't really matter. Pour the water on. Add the right amount of milk for you, then take a teaspoon, squeeze the bag against the side of the mug and in one deft move, flip the teabag into the bin or compost. Stir the tea and tap the teaspoon against the edge of the mug. Don't try to multi-task. Maybe tap your fingers on the countertop.

As these instructions indicate, the fundamentals of pottering are:

Make do with what you've got (tea, milk, water, mug, teaspoon)

—

Don't try too hard (note the lack of ceremony)

—

Movement (admittedly not a lot)

—

Keep it local (you're not going very far)

—

Keep it digital-free (virtual tea is pointless)

Right, now that's sorted, let's take these principles and look at each one closely.

Make do with what you've got

Pottering teaches you to be resourceful and develops your skills in compromise and improvisation. If you're making tea and you haven't got any tea, have a coffee instead, or another drink. Whatever you've got in your cupboard. If for some reason your kettle is out of action, boil the water in a pan. No milk? Use a slice of lemon as they do in Russia, where milk in tea is not a thing. Not only does pottering teach you to be resourceful, but also it can lead to entirely new experiences.

Don't try too hard

There are millions of ways to make a cup of tea. So many decisions: water temperature (boiling versus wait a bit), receptacle (cup and saucer, mug, teapot), milk amount and order (first or last; splash, glug or not at all), tea selection (fruit, herbal, green, different types of black tea: Assam versus English Breakfast, even though they are almost the same thing) and brewing time (somewhere on the spectrum between 'forgot about the teabag, but it's still warm, so you might as well otherwise it would be a waste' and 'just *dip* the bag, really quickly, *dip it*, I mean, just show the bag to the water. In fact, let me do it. I'll make the tea').

Consider the words that define pottering 'without definite plan or purpose'. Let those words really sink in and sense the freedom that they imply. You have the freedom to make tea any way you like. You be you. No one is going to judge. It's just you and the tea.

Movement

Pottering implies moving from one activity to another. It is not still. However, you don't have to move far, or fast. There is no destination, distance to be travelled or physical goal. There are no triathlons involved: strain, breathlessness and sweating are unnecessary.

Nevertheless, don't stop moving altogether or you will lose momentum. If you feel you are coming to the end of one pottering activity, think for a moment, sigh, and say out loud, 'Now. What was I doing?' Pause, and a good idea about what to do next will definitely occur to you. If it doesn't, go for a sit and a think.

Keep it local

Being at home is comforting and easy. Don't feel you need to leave the house. However, a lot of pleasure can be derived from wandering down to the shops (not the Big Shops, just the nearest ones). Perhaps 'go for a bit of a drive', but don't have a destination in mind or overdo it distance-wise.

Keep it digital-free

A 24-hour box-set marathon on the sofa is not pottering. Chillaxing with your phone is not pottering. You are certainly occupied, but somehow the pull of social media, the demands of keeping pace with the latest series and the fear of missing out can make you feel empty and completely overwhelmed. What a poor state of affairs that is.

First let's give you some freedom to let go of all that pressure. Take note that with pottering you are usually doing just one thing at a time, so you can't be on social media as well. Pottering has saved you from social media!

Plus, pottering activities are often so inconsequential that you're unlikely to want to tell your social networks about them. Think about it. Are you going to post a picture of yourself organizing and folding all your plastic grocery bags and placing them into one grab-and-go 'best' plastic bag that stays by the front door, ready for your weekly shop? Probably not. (Though if you do, for celebrating the mundane, you are to be commended.) Has Kim Kardashian ever posted a picture of herself standing on a chair flicking a tea towel at a cobweb on the ceiling? No, she has not. Has Cristiano Ronaldo shared a video of himself wiping up toast crumbs from a kitchen table with a damp cloth? That hasn't happened.

Take away the reasons for checking your device. Get a wristwatch and you won't need to look at your phone to find out the time. Write important dates on a calendar and put it somewhere where you can see it. Enjoy 'in-between' time by having a look out of a window.

Should pottering meet all five of these principles?

Take away movement, and you have relaxing. If you were allowed to be digital, would you really potter at all? And if you had to try too hard, travel far or make a special effort, it would create too much stress; thus you would lose all the benefits of a rested mind.

So ideally, yes, meeting all five of these principles would be great, but honestly, there's no pressure. If pottering were to be presented as a business model, it would be a lopsided pentagon sketched out on the back of an envelope.

Make do with what you've got

When you potter, you take pleasure in small things: you don't need any special equipment. Making do with what you have is about living simply. Plus you can become incredibly resourceful when your options are limited. 'Hacks' arise out of a situation when someone was making do. Are you finding that your scourer is inadequate for the task of cleaning around the knobs on your kitchen stove? Poke about in those elusive grooves with a wooden toothpick. Lost your measuring tape? Make do with a piece of string and a ruler. It may take a while to take measurements, but it's better than not being able to do it at all.

In Italy, in the south in particular, they acknowledge the slight ridiculousness of making do with the practice of *l'arte dell'arrangiarsi*, which means 'the art of arranging yourself'. This sounds like a society finishing-school technique that instructs you to sit prettily while wearing inconceivably uncomfortable yet fashionable clothes. However, what *l'arte dell'arrangiarsi* actually means is, 'I will not be defeated by this situation; I will persevere and I will also have a laugh.' Like creatively making a gazebo out of bin bags, duct tape and bamboo gardening canes.

Do what you were going to do anyway

Pottering is about making the best of your circumstances and the resources you have to hand, which is why so much pottering takes place at home. The distinguishing feature of pottering as opposed to 'jobs around the house' is the slow pace at which you do it. 'Rushing about' from one thing to another is not pottering. If you have to stay in for the day, there is no hurry in anything you do because you have given yourself that uncommon luxury of 'spare time'.

Though you might choose to do things you wouldn't do all that often, like reordering the clothes hangers in your wardrobe so that the hooks all face in the same direction, more often you will be doing a small domestic task that recurs in a regular cycle, a ready source of occupation and inspiration. The fun never stops with pottering jobs.

Take a household task like dealing with clean laundry. Pull it out of the basket in a long, sweet-smelling damp lump. Use a big shirt to make it all into a bundle, tying the arms with the lowermost hem. Carry it to an appropriate airing facility to dry: washing line, radiator, clothes rack. Let your mind wander for a bit. Untangle and sort. Listen out for the satisfying thwap as you shake out each damp towel before hanging it up. There is no need for a 'system': pull each piece of clothing from your bundle or basket and take pleasure from serendipitously finding a pair of nearly matching socks, pegging them together on the line. Think ahead to the clean, dry pillowcases and sheets on your bed. Hmmm, cosy *and* fresh *and* crisp. There's a nice bedtime to look forward to.

As you can see, another distinguishing feature of pottering versus 'jobs around the house' is that it is not a chore and you derive the tiniest bit of satisfaction from doing it.

And the thing is, if you do all the things you need to do, you deserve to have a nice sit down. Time to put the kettle on and remember the pottering basics. Look out of the window and watch your laundry flap elegantly in the wind.

Having a nice sit down

Though you can occupy your hands while sitting – with something like knitting or whittling – sitting down is the one activity that allows you to opt out of the pottering rule on movement, for a while anyway.

Make tea. Find your comfiest chair, ideally with a view, and land your backside into the middle of it, letting out a muffled 'oof' as you do so. Gather your thoughts and sip your tea. Check that you are comfortable. Have a quiet five minutes. If you're in no particular hurry to 'get on' with doing other things, close your eyes for a moment, or read a book. For as long as you like.

Improvisation and compromise

Humans are pragmatic creatures and have been fending for themselves, making do with what they've got, for 100,000 years. You've got this.

What you need and what you want are two very different things. You need warmth, food, shelter and company. You can improvise and compromise on everything else. What you *want* could range from finding a way to deal with the world's most serious problems to a desire for the wallpaper behind the radiator to stick to the wall. You've been ignoring it even though it's peeling away and has been annoying you for ages.

With the scenarios 'solve all the world's problems' and 'stick peeling wallpaper to wall', what you have is an illustration of two points on a scale of achievability and a demonstration of your degree of control. On your own, you are not going to transform the world into a utopia (although we can all try to do our bit). In the meantime, it's certainly within your power to find something with the right amount of tackiness for minor DIY jobs. You don't need wallpaper paste, PVA glue or even a glue stick, honestly: Cornflakes and milk would do, or any other combination of carbs and sugars with adhesive qualities.

Improvisation and compromise like this prove how capable you really are. Practise making do with what you've got daily and you'll soon be an expert in both.

Rummaging

Compromise and improvise when you can, but sometimes you will need to find the exact thing you need for a job. 'Finding a thing' will inevitably lead you to rummaging: in drawers, cupboards and the peripheries of your living space like a shed or garage. It will be an item you don't often have a need for (and you have consequently put it away) but is extremely handy for a specific use, like a gadget that hulls strawberries or a hand tool such as a bradawl (a pokey woodworking implement that makes a tiny hole in preparation for a nail or screw).

While rummaging for the thing you're looking for, you'll also rediscover useful things you had forgotten you had: a mini screwdriver to fix glasses, that came out of a Christmas cracker; a cocktail shaker; a book on identifying insects. You'll find useful bits and bobs in a receptacle such as a jam jar at the back

of a desk drawer containing a set of compasses and a treasury tag (a short length of string with a metal or plastic end that is threaded through a hole in a set of papers and keeps them together). A tin, in a kitchen drawer, rumbles pleasingly as you knock it because it contains a collection of random metal: staples and paper clips, padlocks, differently sized screws and a squashed ball of wire.

Sometimes you don't know quite what you need, but you can rummage anyway: in obscure corners of your home, toolboxes, the loft and the cupboard under the stairs, at the back of the wardrobe, in decorative trinket boxes, hiding places and a dish in the hallway by the door. It's not just coins from overseas and keys from (sometimes) unknown locks in that dish. It contains all the things that have been decanted from a pocket: a stray Lego brick, a souvenir holiday magnet, a single bead.

When you come across something that might be useful, do one of two things: either leave it exactly where it is, even if it's a bit random, or relocate it to exactly the right place. Warning: make this a sensible relocation, as putting it 'somewhere safe' could mean you will never, ever see it again. So, on second thoughts, the best option is just to leave it where it is, thus preserving the pottering 'rummaging cycle' (lost it, look for it, found it, repeat).

Moving things around

Even though a good principle to live by is to leave things where they are, feel free to reorder, relocate, adjust and tidy as you will. Take a cutlery drawer, for example. Decant all spoons, knives, forks, peculiar utensils and old Prosecco corks. Extract the cutlery tray, tip it upside down and bang it over the sink. Put everything back into some sort of order, minus the fluff and crumbs.

As for things out on display – a vase or a plant, for example – try out new positions. Shift them slightly along the shelf. Relocate them to the mantelpiece. Move them to a different room. 'Style' and 'curate' groups of items. See what could do with a change and a new look. Put things back where they should go.

When you have *a lot* of time on your hands, you could alphabetize your books or reorder them according to the colour of their spines so that they look elegantly co-ordinated on the shelf. Only do this if you like doing that kind of thing. Don't feel you have to.

The store cupboard

A key principle of making do is having store-cupboard 'staples' and then using what you've got to come up with a tasty meal seemingly out of nothing. Store-cupboard ingredients include things like rice or flour and are generally foodstuffs that don't go off for a while: dry goods (dried beans, sugar), long-life packets (jelly, gravy granules), tins (baked beans, pineapple) or pre-serves and pickles like jam and piccalilli.

Celebrity chefs would have you believe that store-cupboard ingredients include sumac and preserved lemons. You do not need these. All credit to those who are making our lives more exotic with a dish-enhancing ingredient such as pomegranate molasses. However, you will almost certainly never get round to using it. You may feel you should try to put it in everything for a while to 'use it up', but it doesn't go in anything you usually make, like pasta sauce or sandwiches. Realistically it's a thing you put in the cupboard, feel guilty about not using, eventually forget about and then – when it is four years past its expiry date – chuck out. It's easy to go on the same journey with sushi kits. They seem like a good idea. You would like to gain a reputation for sushi-making among friends, and sushi seems like a simple and healthy option, but in the end, you realize that a sushi kit is a little intimi-dating, even though the kit itself has 'easy-to-follow' instructions. Every time you spot the unopened box in your cupboard, you can feel like you have ever so slightly failed. Slide it to the back of the cupboard out of sight, then chuck it out, as above, later.

Don't buy slightly useless ingredients in the first place. Instead, make do with what you've got. Go to your fridge, open the door, look briefly inside. Open each of the kitchen cupboards one by one,

and have a quick look. Here's where you can be particularly resourceful. What have you got that would make a meal? A baked potato with tuna and cheese, an omelette, or pasta with pesto can all be made with real store cupboard ingredients. A 'capsule' store-cupboard, if you will – like a capsule wardrobe, but more nourishing. A capsule store cupboard will contain pasta, rice, pesto, eggs, jam, bread, fruit, onions, frozen berries, frozen corn, frozen spinach, fish fingers, frozen fish fillets, canned tomatoes and canned beans. If you are running low on these and there is nothing in your fridge at all, you will have to venture out to the local shop (see Chapter 5: Keep it local). (If you really want to learn how to make sushi, learn something new and go on a course – see Chapter 7: The pottering year. Then you'll find out how to make sushi from someone who knows what they're doing and can be encouraging.)

Why are you pottering?

Pottering provides you with 'something to do'. Learn about your motivations and ask yourself: why are you pottering? Do you need a brief distraction? Are you procrastinating or avoiding doing something? Are you trying to look busy, thus preventing someone from asking you to do something? Are you taking it easy for a while?

Do you simply need something to do because you have to stay in for the day? Take being at home to wait for a delivery, for example. You are informed that it will come 'between nine and four', i.e. the best part of the day. 'Got to wait in for a delivery', you sigh to friends, who nod and sympathize. However, on the inside you're really looking forward to seven hours of being at home with not much to do. When your ambition is slight and your requirements are limited, making do with what you've got really keeps the pressure off.

You don't need a reason to take some time back, and there is no need to overthink it. Remember that pottering is activity without plan or purpose, so by its nature it is one of the most spontaneous things you can do. And as everyone knows, spontaneity is exciting.

Don't try too hard

Making do with what you've got means accepting that you don't always have to strive for perfection. Pottering is a pause in the day. It's a mental break. You have opted out of the tyranny of pressure.

Life can feel too busy, with a constant stream of too much activity. *Even at weekends.* By taking a chance to potter, which is entirely optional, we regain the tiniest bit of control. It's as if we're able to trick ourselves for a moment that we have *so much* time we can afford to do something trivial. It's a small act of rebellion. This is especially true when we don't try too hard: not doing a thorough job of picking the bobbles off a jumper will always be fine. It will look better than it did (and you can pick off a few more another time).

If pottering were an outdoor pursuit, it wouldn't be an endurance test; you wouldn't have to get a good time; you don't even have to try your best. It's a pootle around the park for the sake of feeling the fresh air on your face.

Flexibility

Pottering is a flexible activity that exists on a spectrum of thoroughness. Pottering can take a moment (flicking crumbs off a tablecloth), or you could spend weeks doing it (discovering new places as you wander along a coastal walk on holiday).

Filling the time available is another aspect, so that if pottering were plotted on a graph, with one axis denoting 'doing a thorough job' and the other axis denoting 'time available', it would look different depending on who you are and the way you like to apply yourself. There is no single way of doing pottering. For those who like to stick to one thing at a time, there might be a continuous upward line indicating productivity – and if that's how you like to relax, that is absolutely the way to apply yourself to pottering. If, however, you are someone who starts a job and, after a while, switches to another, or stops for a cup of tea, does a bit more then pauses to answer the door because a delivery arrives, which leads you to open a parcel, consider the contents, dispose of the packaging and forget about what you were doing in the first place, that is fine too (for more on this, see Chapter 4: Movement). In this second scenario the line on the graph might be very short and it wouldn't be continuous. In graphical terms, it wouldn't look as though you had done all that much, but in fact

you would have completed a lot of small tasks, achieving restful 'flow' and leading to an entirely different visual diagram.

The contrariness of pottering

Entirely simultaneously, these two contradictory facts are true: everyone is an expert potterer, and no one is an expert potterer because it is not something that you can be an expert in. You can do it frequently, but there is no such thing as 'doing it well'. There are no benchmarks for success. In your own mind, you can be confident about your ability and no one can challenge your 'commitment' or 'attainment'.

You can take pride in everything you do, but no one is judging your performance when you find a matching lid and plastic pot in the odd assortment of containers you use for freezing leftover food. It's just not something you can 'excel' at.

Small jobs

One of the basic guiding principles of pottering is 'don't try too hard', not 'don't try at all': it is not 'sitting about in your onesie on your phone'. The very opposite, in fact. Pottering is relaxing *because* you are occupied. That's why movement (see Chapter 4) and keeping it digital-free (see Chapter 6) are so important.

What is also important is that you *like doing what you're choosing to do when you potter*. A certain degree of satisfaction can be derived from light domestic and DIY tasks, and everyone will be different. If you don't like vacuuming, then – for you – that's not pottering. If you do like pairing socks, then – for you – that is.

Take washing the dishes by hand as an example of something nice and satisfying.

Fill a sink with water, sticking your finger in the water flow to check the temperature. Glance up and around you. Add washing-up liquid and swish to create maximum bubble height. Pause. Watch the water going into the sink. Check water temperature again. Collect items to be washed. Flick bits and crumbs into the bin. Dip each thing in the water, starting with the items that are the least dirty, and scrub or wipe. Rinsing is optional, as is shaking off drips.

Don't feel the need to dry and put away everything. Perhaps leave it where it is for now and come back to put it away later.

Domestic and DIY jobs tend to be useful, so one of the benefits of doing something small is that, though you are making only minimal effort, you will look as if you're being useful. This means that by and large, people will leave you alone to get on with it. That is worth noting if your aim is avoiding someone asking you to do something. There are all manner of things that fall into this category:

Sweep with a broom

You don't have to do this particularly well or thoroughly. Do what you can get away with. If you are sweeping outside, for example, you can shift most of the pile of detritus into the street, or into a flowerbed.

—

Leave something to soak

Such as a pan with particularly stubborn, baked-on jagged brown bits or an item of pale clothing you dropped ketchup on. After a few hours, scrape the bits off the pan and really squeeze your laundry and wring out the water. Soaking is extremely adjustable, based on whether or not you've forgotten about it – as little as half an hour, as much as 48.

—

Sorting

Clean out a bag. Expel the contents and organize into piles implying a destination: put in the bin, put somewhere else, put back in the bag. Dispose of the fragments of paper and particles of dust that have accrued. Pocket the change (assuming it's yours).

—

Fixing

Sew on a button or execute a minor repair on clothing. Attach loops to towels to make them easier to hang on a hook on the back of the bathroom door.

'Specialist' cleaning

Remove the glass dome from a light fitting, tip out the dust and dead insects, and give it a wipe with a cloth.

—

Check over

Oil the moving parts of a bicycle. Upturn the bike and spin the pedals and wheels.

Doing things that are quite satisfying and useful only by the tiniest margin

Some pottering activities can be so undemanding that they are useful only in the loosest possible terms, but doing them is restful and restorative.

Start a button, bits and other gubbins jar. There should definitely be a safety pin and a curtain hook in it. Every time you find a stray or spare button, put it in the jar.

—

Turn your old envelopes into usefully sized scrap paper. Fold, crease and cut with a sharp knife or letter opener. Keep together with a bulldog clip.

—

Arrange fruit in a bowl.

—

Plump up pillows (completely optional on so many levels, but quite a good idea if you need to express some emotion. Bang them hard).

Fill a pepper grinder with peppercorns; put coffee in a decorative canister.

−

Tighten screws that have come a little loose. Glue something.

−

Do one of those tilting games where you have to get ball bearings to rest in a small dip in a maze. When you tilt it too far, one of the ball bearings escapes and you have to incline it the other way.

−

Play the card game patience with a real pack of cards. If you are stuck, you can sneak a peek at cards that are face down. Or do a 1,000-piece jigsaw puzzle.

The cascade effect of pottering

Tiny jobs create further pottering opportunities, leading to a cascade of other mini-jobs.

For example, you might decide that your medical kit needs to be tidied. Giving it a good look over, you see that the kitchen scissors have made their way into it. You were wondering where they were and you've been doing all your usual snipping jobs, like cutting string, with a knife, which doesn't work as well and feels dangerous. Relocate the scissors to the right place.

In your medical kit you have three open packets of throat lozenges. Gather them all and put them in the box that is least squashed. Pair the two thermometers you own: one that you use the most and a spare that you don't like so much.

For an inexplicable reason, your medical kit is also the place you keep your torch, perhaps because you've unconsciously classified it as an 'emergency item' like insect repellent and an arm sling that you have never, ever used.

The torch has no batteries and so you find a pen and begin a to-do list by writing 'buy batteries'. Further exploration reveals that a packet of cold remedy is out of date, so you add that to the list.

At this point you decide that popping out to the chemist, to dispose of old medicines and acquire new supplies, is the best excuse you've had all day to leave the house. This leads you to another pottering principle: 'movement'.

4

Movement

Do you find yourself doing something small ahead of doing something important? With each tiny task it's as if you are mentally preparing, saying to yourself, 'When I've done this trivial thing, over which I have complete control, I'll be ready for anything that's important. I'll be able to concentrate.' You feel as if you cannot start, for example, filling in your passport form until you have wiped down the kitchen countertops and emptied the bin. You're setting easy targets for yourself, in readiness for the more difficult task ahead. You may even find yourself breaking off from something important, like revising for an exam, to wander into the garden to check over and water your flowers. At that moment, getting up, moving, stretching and doing something legitimate feels like the break you need to allow yourself so that you can get back to revising and concentrating again. Movement is a key component of this.

Equally, there are times when you feel as if you are compelled to move – after a party, for example, you find yourself clearing up, even though you could leave it until the morning. Tidying like this somehow helps you to wind down and relax, and get ready for bed.

Achieving flow

Life in Finland isn't all saunas, or hikes in the beautiful outdoors. Some people opt for an evening of extreme rest and relaxation instead. *Kalsarikänni* and *päntsdrunk* are Finnish words to describe 'drinking in your pants on your own with no intention of going out'.

Pottering is often solitary like *päntsdrunk*, but you don't have to get obliterated on booze; in fact, you don't have to drink alcohol at all. Pottering isn't quite so undressed, either – or so still, as movement is very much a factor. It is this movement while doing something the tiniest bit useful that can help you to empty your mind – much like tai chi or meditation. You might feel a restorative benefit while popping out for a length of pipe-lagging for an outdoor tap, for example. (Though this is not something you can spend a weekend doing at a retreat, like tai chi.)

Additionally, with pottering you never, ever have to do it well. Indeed, it is difficult to distinguish between good pottering and not-so-good pottering. Even when you're doing something that is both beneficial and relaxing, like yoga, you know that having your thoughts take a distracted, fidgety turn means

that it's not having the effect it is supposed to be having. ('OK, eyes closed, and now, empty my mind …
[immediately begin to run through things you need to
do] … This mat smells, my face is on a smelly mat …
[initiate list of anxieties … open eyes] That woman's
got a nice top. I should get more Lycra …')

There is no pressure or commitment to pottering;
you don't need anyone to guide you, and therefore there
is no one to judge. The benefits of using pottering to
achieve flow are a) you can choose to do anything in any
order among tasks that you would do anyway, b) you
don't need to practise, c) you don't need any equipment
or to go anywhere specific to do it and d) you can lose
yourself entirely while doing something as mundane as
sorting the recycling or washing the windows.

The movement of pottering can help you discipline
your wandering thoughts, because pottering is flow
itself, with one activity intersecting with another, so:

Get laundry out of the machine

–

Make a bundle

–

Put the bundle on a chair

–

See milk drips on the kitchen surface

–

Put the kettle on for tea

Notice a stray sock that has separated itself from
the laundry pile

—

Wipe away milk drips

—

Kettle has boiled, make tea

—

Put spoon in the sink

—

See indeterminate bits on the floor

—

Put the sock with the rest of the washing

—

Take the washing outside to hang up

—

Notice that your garden path could do with a sweep

—

Fill the watering can

—

Hang out the washing

—

Water the plants

—

Go back inside to get your tea

—

Wash up the spoon

—

Drink tea

Pottering is not necessarily the most efficient course of action to get things done. Notice how the sequence of events is not tidy or predictable. You do not necessarily finish one task before starting another. You do something (put spoon in sink) and then come back to it (wash up spoon). Take note also that while you may see that something needs doing, you ignore it and don't necessarily do it there and then. This approach might be described as 'unordered' pottering.

Doing a sequence of tiny household tasks like this, you can get into a meditative state. You could say that the contemplative, rhythmic nature of pottering is similar to a gymnastics or dance routine. When put together the sequence seems graceful – elegant, even. It's difficult to say whether or not you reach a state of *transcendental* meditation if you're removing lint from a dryer, or putting bottles in your bathroom cabinet in height order, but when you achieve flow while pottering, you are absorbed in a task and, because there are no demands upon you, you can achieve a sense of freedom. Being absorbed and being free are two states of being that can certainly be restful and make you feel content.

Interruptions

Disrupting that contented feeling is perhaps why interruptions during pottering feel uncomfortable. In theory, being interrupted shouldn't be a problem, because you'll often break off and come back to things while pottering, but bizarrely, when you are in a state of pottering flow, an interruption can cause a sensation of intrusion akin to when someone turns a light off and you're still in the room. Remember that there is no pressure with pottering, so unless the interruption is important, you can get back to whatever it was you were doing and finish it.

Orderly pottering

It can be difficult to make sense of other people's routines and rituals. Some people find it utterly infuriating to break off one thing before it's quite finished, and move on to something else. It is especially incomprehensible for those who like to take a logical approach. Luckily, because there is no prescriptive method or standardized format for pottering, it needn't be chaos. You might be more comfortable with 'orderly' pottering, where you have the freedom to be tidy and thorough. This is where, for a while, you are absorbed in doing one thing only. You finish, and follow it with something else.

For example: do one hour of weeding in the garden. Wash your hands. Get changed out of your gardening clothes. Sit down and read an entire newspaper. Finish the newspaper and fold it. Decide that it is time for lunch. Get up and head for the kitchen.

What happens when you're pottering like this is that you're occupied with a series of discrete activities, none of which makes too many demands of you. You're occupied enough not to think about anything too complicated. There is no hurry to do each one of the tasks and so, although you're 'busy' in the loosest possible terms, you're not rushed.

Focusing on one thing

Focused pottering really comes into its own when you are doing a task on a big scale, such as clearing out a large cupboard.

To start with, open the doors of the cupboard and survey the magnitude of the task. Begin with the easiest shelf or corner. This is usually at eye level and is the place where you have recently shoved something to get it out of sight. Alternatively, it is the go-to corner in which you know where everything is. Start there and you will gradually clear space. As you go, put actual rubbish in bin bags. Everything else can go into one of four mental zones: 'belongs somewhere else', 'goes back in the cupboard', 'I don't know what to do with it' and 'might come in handy one day'. Within the 'belongs somewhere else' category is recycling and stuff to give away. When everything is out of the cupboard, you may have four neat piles or you may be surrounded by what looks like utter chaos. It doesn't matter. Put away the things that belong elsewhere, and put everything else back in the cupboard in some semblance of order. Justify not making a decision there and then about the two piles 'I don't know what to do with it' and 'might come in handy one day', because you will come back to it at some point in the future.

DIY

Taking your time, listening to the radio and stopping frequently for a break is a pottering approach you take when you're wallpapering a room or tiling a bathroom. (Note: this leisurely attitude will prove hugely inconvenient to the rest of the household, and the equipment required will almost certainly 'get in the way'.)

Hobbies

You might only ever potter doing one single thing. You have a hobby such as crochet or upholstery. It's *your* thing and it is ideal because it's something you can break off from and pick up again. Choose your specialist area wisely. It will have to be something that you love: mid-century furniture, Italian motorbikes or the restoration of a Victorian greenhouse. Don't forget that hobbies that need paraphernalia are especially good for pottering because you can spend a lot of time collecting and sorting through the things you need. There is potentially a lot of gadgetry involved in everything from coffee-making to film photography to making home-brew.

You might want to 'give something a go' just the once. Try candle-making or making flavoured gin. It doesn't necessarily have to be done well. Do it once, so you can say you've done it and then try something else, like making a croquembouche (one of those showpiece towering bakery concoctions of choux pastry and caramel). Doing something physical creates a sense of achievement because you have something tangible to show for your efforts.

And then there are other activities – those which may never come to a definite end because they're a lifelong endeavour, like the interminable quest to restore a vintage car. When you dismantle the car, you can take pleasure in taking notes, labelling items and placing each part in boxes 'somewhere safe', which means inevitably that you will have to rummage for them later. The achievement here comes in tiny increments: finding the correct lightbulb, restoring the leather steering wheel, treating bodywork for rust and so on.

Restoring a vintage car necessitates acquiring several new skills. Along the way you will find out about mechanics, electronics and welding. You will travel to specialist shops for all the bits and tools you require; you will be compelled to go to sales just to see if they've got the specific thing you're looking for. Your passion will provide you with anecdotes and tips, and throughout, you will meet liked-minded people, with whom you'll have plenty to discuss and share.

Going a short distance

The ebb and flow of pottering activities sometimes requires you to 'pop out' to get or do something, like getting a pair of shoes re-heeled or going to the local shop to get bin bags.

Popping out for something is as much about getting a change of scene as it is about actually needing something. If you are in a state of pottering flow, it might, admittedly, take you a while to leave the house. By all means stay at home and potter if that's what you would like to do. There is no pressure to be too adventurous, and being a little reclusive is fine for a while. However, it is worth knowing that procrastination is definitely a characteristic of pottering (for ways to deal with procrastination, see Chapter 8: 'Planning' and achievement). You may need to go out and get something eventually. Finish what you're doing or make an attempt to break off, leaving things where they are, and go.

While you are out, as you are passing the post office, you realize that you need to send a birthday card. You go into the post office to get stamps. You head home, choose a card and write it, leaving it by the front door so that you can post it the next time you pop out. You were thinking of getting an impromptu haircut later and that would be the perfect opportunity.

Going further afield

Do you love public transport for all that it represents as a reasonably priced, convenient way to travel with fellow humans? Or do you dislike it intensely because it represents crowded, loud and slightly smelly journeys to school or work? In case it is possible to sway your opinion: travelling on public transport during the day when few people are around is much nicer than using a bus or train at either end of the day, when most people commute. People are slower and much more polite. On buses you'll see that your fellow passengers are regulars who nod to each other as they board. On trains you'll see that people will move their belongings and smile as you sit next to them. It is quite a different experience outside rush hour. Even if travelling by public transport will take you a while, waiting can teach you patience, and anyway, on a pottering day you are free from the constraints of time. Embrace the extra time it will take and use the journey to alternate between looking out of the window and observing your fellow passengers. What do you notice about the scenes that pass you by? What can you learn about the people around you? Through observation, could you – like super-sleuth Sherlock Holmes – come up with a feasible backstory about each one of them?

The more time you have, the further you can go and the more interesting your journey can be. Travelling by public transport allows you to go somewhere that is far enough away to be unfamiliar to you and can therefore seem much more exotic than your immediate local area. Getting off a bus at any point along a route gives you a sense of freedom and presents you with a huge range of possibilities.

Going out for the day

You don't need a specific plan; you need a *vague* plan. In this context, vague is good. Start with a general direction, such as going 'into town' or 'to the countryside'. You don't even need to have a destination in mind, as the journey is just as much a legitimate activity as going somewhere specific. Let serendipity take you and follow the signs.

Pottering *somewhere* for the day presents all sorts of opportunities: going to an exhibition at a museum and then setting one or two postcards straight in the shop afterwards, or spontaneously going into a cafe you don't know. You can discover and explore an area you've never been to before and appreciate a new sight: a local market, a pretty street, a beautiful field, a spectacular sky.

Prepare a picnic for your day out by opening your fridge and cupboards and selecting from what's in there. If all you've got is apples and nuts, that's your picnic (see Chapter 2: Make do with what you've got).

You might choose to go out for 'a bit of a drive'. Find your keys, get in the car, tap the steering wheel with your index fingers and exhale loudly. Going for a drive needn't be a cinematic-scale epic road trip; you might decide to take your bicycle out of the garage instead. Set off for somewhere that you have heard of but never been to – somewhere that's supposed to nice. Or spontaneously decide to do something you have not done for a while, like going for an ice cream at the seaside.

Keep it local

Keeping it local is as much about a state of mind and a sense of community as it is about convenience. The southern African word *ubuntu* alludes to this: it means 'I am because we are'. When you take a short walk to pop out for something you start to become interconnected with the people around you: your neighbours, local businesses and people walking their dogs.

Why are you going out? That's not an accusation, but a genuine query. Are you on a mini-mission to get something specific? Or are you going for a wander and a change of scene?

Checking the weather
There's no need to look on your phone to see what the weather is going to be like because a) you are not going out for long and b) you are not going very far.

The very best way of finding out about the weather is to open your front door and use your judgement. Pick up on visual clues from other people – is someone wearing a warm coat or carrying an umbrella? What usually happens at this time of year? What happened yesterday?

Feel the temperature and movement of air on your skin and then look up at the sky. If the sky is dark grey and angry-looking and it seems really quite blowy, shut the door and leave it for a bit. However, if the sky is grey and there is a breeze, you might need your coat. Even if it does rain and you don't have an umbrella or a hood on your coat, improvise: shelter at a bus stop, in a shop or at the library. If it feels hot and the sky is a vivid blue, with lovely puffy clouds, you may need a hat and some sunscreen – and on the way back, get yourself an ice cream. Before you set out, don't forget to rummage in the dish by the door for your keys.

The local shop

Ideally your local shop is six minutes' walk away – tops. That way you can be there and back again within 15 minutes. If you're lucky, it's so close you can get away with going there in your slippers. Take a bag with you, even if you're just popping there for a newspaper. Inspiration may strike and you could find yourself impulse-buying string, envelopes and blank invoice books, which – inexplicably – such shops always sell.

The primary benefit of a local shop is to be reassuring. It's there to provide basics such as milk and bread, emergency 'filling' foods such as potatoes and sage-and-onion stuffing (for when guests drop by unexpectedly and you need to expand the meal to accommodate them), and freeze-dried and sealed foods to which you just add water. These are never nice.

The area in which the corner shop excels is the emergency tea party: there are 41 cakes to choose from (no exaggeration, go to yours and count them), 34 types of biscuit, *all* the chocolate, loads of different savoury snacks, seven kinds of ice cream, ice-cream cones, everything you need to make a cake, all the cake accessories (candles, a frill, decorations), and niche and retro sugary treats such as Iced Gems, Family Circle and fig rolls. There are also provisions for the savoury side of an emergency party (bread, spread, ham, cheese, tuna, jam). Don't forget an extra pint or two of milk, because your unexpected guests will be drinking tea.

Other shops

They are sometimes hard to find, and a little further away than the local shop, but if you are really lucky you will have a surviving independent specialist shop nearby. Books, kitchenware, ironmongery, whatever it is, with the artisan wares they sell and the original shop fittings, these places are undeniably photogenic.

Don't just pop in and capture its charm in a photo to post on your social-media feed. Buy something. Anything. And keep going back.

Imagine that shop was a critically endangered species like a polar bear, only it was living on a high street near you and you had the means to keep it alive. You want those shops there because they make your local area interesting. Plus you can stock up on things that you can't get anywhere else. Find a way to make it a part of your life. Make a habit of buying presents there or find another reason to go in fairly regularly and buy something. An artisan deli is not a food gallery, it is a business and its customers help it to survive.

Local shops that have survived high-street Armageddon are still going for one of three reasons, all connected with the people who run them – who know everything there is to know about their chosen specialist area:

They are very reliable, having everything you could possibly want (in an ironmonger's that would be a monkey-tail window stay, a set of pulleys for a washing line and screws sold singly).

—

They are experts in 'ordering something in' (in a deli this would be canned tomatoes grown in alluvial soil, gluten-free mince pies and a bulk order of dried mango).

The shop is fronted by someone with the charm and presence of a Hollywood A-lister. Spending a few moments with this person is a joy and an education, and such is their charisma that you'll come away actually feeling better about yourself.

An intrinsic component of visiting the local shop is passing the time of day with the person behind the counter. As time goes on and your visits become regular, you will get to know them better and these encounters will become longer. Begin by saying hello as you arrive; as you depart, raise a hand in acknowledgement and wish them well. Try out this unusual level of friendliness in the Big Shops too. It will completely freak them out.

The local vicinity

'The shops' is just one place in your neighbourhood where people gather. Consider the library, the post office, the pub, the cafe. You might even have a local community centre. Maximize opportunities for expanding your local horizons by passing through these places: take out books from the library and return them regularly; join a local evening class to learn something new (see Chapter 7: The pottering year). Pop to the shop for a magazine. Seek out a bench and take the time to read the dedication on it. Sit, look through your magazine and have a think in the fresh air.

Milk delivery

Consider the life cycle of the milk round: somewhere not too far away a whole tanker of milk is distributed into individual glass bottles, sealed, crated and loaded on to milk floats, slow electric vehicles that travel with a sedate hum. A milk delivery person, who is prepared to get up and start work *at 2 am*, sets off from a depot and drops off pints of milk and other basic groceries. It's a fully personalized distribution service: full-fat, semi or skimmed, other dairy goods, non-dairy alternatives like 'vegan cheese', juice and bread, with an expanding portfolio of locally produced and artisan foods, if you're lucky.

The very best thing about getting your milk delivered is 'rinsing and returning'. Don't cheat by putting your bottles in the dishwasher. Wash them, by hand. Put a small amount of water in the bottle, slosh the water around, put your hand over the top, shake it up and down, upturn the bottle, glugging the water out, then head for your doorstep and put out the bottle with a 'plink', ready for the milkman/milkwoman to pick it up and take it back to the depot. Obviously, saving the planet one non-plastic bottle at a time is good, but witnessing this beautiful, regular and cyclical process is what's in it for you. So satisfying.

Don't forget to pass the time of day with the milkman when he knocks on your door for payment. Also don't forget that you may need to pay in cash.

The neighbours

Putting the milk bottles out provides you with the perfect opportunity for an encounter with the neighbours. (Putting out the bins and sweeping the front step also work in this regard.) It begins with eye contact and a nod, moves on with speed to a cheerful 'Morning!' and a wave, and before long you're knocking on each other's doors to pop in for a chat and going to the local pub quiz together. You have found people, close by, that you can rely on. Invaluable.

6

Keep it digital-free

Epicurus, the Greek philosopher who introduced the world to the notion of hedonism, asserted that pleasure was the ultimate goal, but should not be sought through an excess of everything pleasurable. Instead, he believed happiness came from a simple life, preferring a nice chat with friends over too much excitement. Doing this, he believed, brings tranquillity and contentment. Talking with friends, being with people and getting out in your community are certainly antidotes to loneliness and isolation.

Too much of anything is not good for us, especially when it cuts us off from people – as some digital services and devices do. Take relaxing while watching a box set. You're on the second season and it's only when you think 'This should be coming to an end now' that you check how many more episodes there are. There are another six, and each one is 45 minutes. The show is OK, but that's another four and a half hours of your life. You've already seen season one (eight hours), and the first half of season two is making you feel like you're committed now, but you haven't seen any of your friends in a while and you just wish it wasn't going to take so much time to finish it. There are seasons three, four and five to go and you're wondering which ones are worth skipping and whether it counts as 'watching' if you simply catch the gist of the whole thing at triple speed.

Watching a box set isn't so relaxing after all. Honestly, switch it off and do something else instead.

All too much

Much like a modern-day Swiss Army knife, digital services and devices are useful multi-tools, helping us with banking and navigating journeys and managing our diaries. And yet, despite all that ability to organize our time, it can feel as if we cannot acquire a single moment to be tranquil.

Though digital services often afford convenience, paradoxically the more time we spend in a digital sphere, the less time we have. Devices give us too much to do and multiple things to check, requiring you always to be 'on'. Looking at a social-media feed takes up an inordinate amount of time. A thirst for the new keeps you looking at various feeds. You spend time looking for something interesting, but anything genuinely gratifying doesn't come along all that often.

The notion of 'too much information' used to mean 'over-sharing the personal stuff', but now it feels as though the words 'too much information' mean exactly that: too much stuff, constantly. All the time.

How many times have you attempted to check something on your phone only for your effort to be derailed by something else? Or failed to look something up or check facts you meant to because you know the answer is there and you can 'check it later'? But you don't. It's as if our phones – which ironically give us access to all the information in the world – are keeping us apart from our natural curiosity.

A digital life is at odds with pottering

Think about all the things you could be doing instead of 'being digital', and consider all the face-to-face conversations you could be having with people you like. Make a list with pen and paper and think how much more satisfying achieving those things would be.

A digital life is at odds with pottering because:

A digital life is not 'doing' enough. Pottering is a verb that is continuous; it implies shifting, physically, between one thing and another.

—

There is not enough variety.
There are too many nagging, fast-paced reminders,

which create too much 'noise'. With the exception of the burble of the radio in the background, pottering is fairly quiet.

Conducting yourself in a way that is incompatible with a digital life is not necessarily a bad thing.

It takes all sorts to make the world. Noticing the differences between oneself and other people is a perfectly natural response to being curious about the world and the different sorts of people who live in it. What is not quite so understandable, when you think about it, is how some people stake their reputations on sneering, sniping and ranting incessantly about how people look and/or are not fitting in precisely with their world view. Witnessing that daily can be incredibly disheartening. When did we lose our ability to be polite? If you potter instead, you won't see any of that nonsense in the first place. You'll discover that pottering is extremely non-judgemental.

In fact, ignoring digital devices and limiting your access to them also means that you are not constantly bombarded with messages, information, unrealistic images of perfection and pictures of social occasions that you haven't been invited to. Without witnessing all of that, you can have some time that is your own, during which someone is not trying to sell you something, show you something pretty, tell you something that's useless and irrelevant – or show how witty and amusing they are.

Social media can also leach into an occasion that should simply be fun. Staging something for a good photo opportunity takes the spontaneity out of it. Imagine you're out for the evening for a nice dinner with friends. Your thoughts flick ahead to how your evening will look on your social-media feeds, and in the back of your mind you're planning the photos and post for maximum impact. Already, even before the photos are posed for and taken, there exists a tiny germ-sized anxiety about how you'll look and how others will see you. Instead, why not enjoy yourself and make a decision not to take a photo?

When you keep it digital-free, you don't have to do something and then arrange it artfully in order to take a picture and make a statement of some sort. Pottering is not often a good photo opportunity. You don't have to be self-conscious. You can just do the thing, enjoy doing it, and then own and enjoy the feeling of how you've spent your time. It's a stream of enjoyment with real people, without interruption. This can be liberating.

Pottering is what you're doing when you're not 'living your best life'. Do yourself a massive favour and step away for a while.

Here's how you can be digital-free. It's a digital detox bucket list.

Seek out people

When you are in the presence of people, you'll discover that they tend to be much more fun and interesting than digital devices. They hug you and smile at you. They may not provide all the answers, but they can be kind and sympathetic and say 'oh dear' when you're feeling fed up about something.

If you are off your devices and in the presence of real people, you will almost certainly receive advice, instructions, reports, tips, ideas for 'looks' and home-spun 'wisdom' from any one of them. It is well meant and is somehow more satisfactory than a constant scroll of words and pictures. It is also a way for people to show they care about you.

Admittedly, those people can also frown at you and look cross, but at least you know where you are and you can ask them, there and then, what's wrong. You're not left with digital silence, wondering what it was that caused someone to switch off from you.

A conversation in person is not a series of witty retorts and one-liners, as it can be on social media. You take turns listening and reacting, so you'll find out just as much about them as they find out about you. And, unlike a search engine, when you ask a question, you may need to wait for a response while the other person thinks about how best to compose their answer, especially if it's a difficult question. In a conversation, you make eye contact and read each other's body language. Compare the dopamine hit of someone liking your post to the pleasure you get when you realize that someone actually likes *you*.

—

Queueing

Are you in no special hurry? In a supermarket, always join the queue for the person at the till rather than the automatic scanner line. Do not look at your phone while in the queue; instead, look about you and take pleasure in the moment you get to first place. Whoop! A queue is a place where everyone takes turns being first. It's a meritocracy where your patience is rewarded in the end.

—

Make a phone call

Before mobile phones were commonplace, you could make calls in three locations: home, office or a telephone box. When mobile phones first became available, they were perceived to be remarkable because you could make a call *wherever you were*. What would be genuinely extraordinary now would be finding and then using a public phone in your local area. That really would be a novelty.

Alternatively, make a call from home on a landline if you have one. Phone someone 'for a chat'. This might feel a bit unnatural at first, intrusive even – especially if you haven't texted them beforehand to tell them that you're going to give them a call. Guaranteed, the first

thing they will say is, 'I thought you were my mum/ grandad' (etc.), because those are the people who call landline numbers. Or cold callers. Which you sort of are, but you're one that friends will want to hear from.

—

Write a letter

Sending a letter presents so many opportunities for the potterer: rummaging in drawers for paper and a pen; the appreciation of the thickness of real writing paper; sitting, thinking and planning what to compose; the act of writing itself; the art of handwriting; the possibility of wandering down to the shops to locate a stamp; the insertion of a precisely folded rectangle of paper into an envelope; more rummaging for an address book; wandering out again to post your letter. Even well-executed letters of complaint present an opportunity to get your thoughts in order and provide you with the satisfaction that you've said what you wanted to say in an elegant way.

Composing a letter, card or note definitely requires effort, but some people truly deserve them. Letters can contain appreciation, thanks and recognition, invitations, expressions of feelings, kindness, condolences, a run-down of what you've been doing and an enquiry about the recipient's wellbeing.

Days later the letter lands on your recipient's doormat. When you send someone a letter, there is none of the instantaneous feedback loop that you get when you send a text. There's no cheery 'thanks' or kiss-kiss emoji, or 'I love you too!' When you send a letter, that's not the kind of gratification you'll get. (Although you could include a stamped self-addressed envelope if you really wanted a reply.)

A letter written by hand can contain important words of love and thanks that might otherwise be left unsaid. The stationery it is written on is a tangible reminder of you for the recipient, and if the words you have written are worth treasuring, the letter will be kept and reread. It creates a lasting impact and is properly memorable.

—

Read a newspaper or magazine

Magazines and newspapers have no infinite scroll. Each one has an end. You can flick through the entire thing, make a mental note of all the articles that look interesting, read them in any order you like, and if there's an advert you are not interested in, you can turn the page over – it doesn't appear incessantly, blinking at you, ever present whenever you try to look at the magazine. There will be things in that magazine that you do not find interesting. Equally, there will be things that you would never otherwise have known were fascinating, but are. And the best thing is that you can nip down to the shop to get one. Many are devoted to hobbies. Go into a newsagent's, stand in front of the selection and pick out the one that looks the most interesting.

Make a photo album

Print out all your favourite photos and put them in a photo album. Then every so often have a good look at it and recall what you liked about the time each picture was taken. Look at it with someone to further explore memories of the times and places when the photos were taken. Dig out your family's old albums. You will notice that before the 1960s everyone is squinting; almost every picture then was taken outside, as that was the only place where you could get good enough light for a photo. And in pictures from the 1960s and 1970s you'll see at least one hideous thing (curtains, haircut, someone smoking far too close to a baby).

–

Telling the time

How many times a day do you look at your phone to check the time, get distracted by the notifications, and then get sucked into checking everything on your phone *except* the time? Avoid this unproductive sequence of events by getting a watch – but not one that monitors your heartbeat, counts the steps you've taken or requires you to shout instructions at it. Just a watch that displays what time it is. For extra non-digital points, get an analogue wind-up watch.

–

Make lists

Keep a paper and pen handy to write down all the things you need to remember and do. You may need a series of lists: things to do today, shopping, people to invite round, books to read, songs you like, a coaching-style overview of your ambitions and life goals. Jot these down on scraps of paper or the back of an envelope and they will feel tangible and achievable.

—

Keep a diary

For a period of time, write down events and thoughts in a notebook. Just a sentence or two. Don't worry if you don't do it every day, or remember everything that happened. It's a record to exercise your memory and provide you with an insight that you can look back on to remember you as you are now. A diary need not start on 1 January, when most printed diaries begin. It does not have to detail all your most secret thoughts. The diary could have a focus, such as a simple list of the books you've read, the food you've eaten or the jobs you've done in the garden.

—

Listen to the radio

Radio is the perfect company for the potterer. Speech radio in particular offers a comforting background noise. It's like having a non-intrusive friend in the room, providing you with entertainment, useful facts and opinions, and dramas (real and fictional). As for music stations, not all tunes will necessarily be to your taste: just wait for the next track to come on or tune in to another station.

Financial transactions

For a local, small 'top-up' shop, add up everything in your head as you go and at the end attempt to assemble the correct coins and notes to pay for your shopping in cash. Or try to pay for something by cheque. Be prepared for confusion and bemusement. If you do manage to pay by cheque, you might have to guide the recipient on what to look out for (correct amount, date, signature).

—

Maps and guidebooks

Maps are a key component of making plans for a day trip or holiday. Have a destination in mind and, without any digital assistance, plan a route to somewhere you have heard is nice, like Frinton or Abergavenny. You may need to start with a national roadmap and look up your destination in the index, which will give you a page number and grid reference. Then, when you get there, acquire a local map so that you can find your way around. Or ask people who look like they're local for directions and recommendations. Instead of relying on your phone to find where you're going, take a note of the address before you go, find the right street and then locate your final destination by looking at the numbers on the buildings.

Plan your trip beforehand by reading a guidebook. Perhaps you can borrow one from the local library.

Write a list of all the places you aim to visit.

Reference books

It starts with wanting to know the difference between one word and another – omnipercipient (perceiving everything) and omnipresence (being everywhere at once) – and goes on to improve your vocabulary: looking up words in a dictionary or thesaurus will make you feel the tiniest bit clever. Note down words you like in a notebook. Dip into other reference books for amusement.

–

Write down recipes

Ask around friends, family and colleagues for their favourite tried-and-tested recipes and write them down in a book. Snip others out of magazines. Write down your own recipe 'accidents' that have turned out well. Borrow books and copy down recipes that look appealing.

Still having difficulty getting off your digital devices?

Distance yourself from all devices for a while. Put them in silent or flight mode somewhere inaccessible. Or give them to someone to look after. Let them run out of charge.

Develop a healthy lack of interest in your phone. Whenever you see it, in your head say, 'I am so bored with you' and regard it as a particularly persistent annoyance. (Which it can be.) Set yourself a time limit for using your phone or limit how you use it (for example, only use your phone for making calls; only pick it up if it rings). Don't take it with you when you go out.

Being digital, if you really must

Though there are quite a few disadvantages to being logged on to an incessant stream of stuff all the time, the colossal convenience and usefulness of some digital services means that going off grid completely for ever can put you at a disadvantage. Even when pottering. Using an app to find out when the next bus is due, for example; looking up how to propagate cuttings; arranging parcel delivery times; and so on. However, it's sensible to limit your use from time to time:

Set rules for yourself about using digital devices – not at mealtimes, not in the company of others, not at bedtime.

–

Switch off all notifications, bleeps and vibrations, and remove all apps you know to be time-consuming.

–

Delete apps you don't use. Delete apps you use rarely. Delete apps that cause you stress and boredom.

–

Find analogue alternatives, if you can, to stop you checking your phone unnecessarily: a calendar, an alarm clock, a radio, a TV, a landline, newspapers, notepad and pen, map and cash. Acquire these and you will be fully equipped for the twentieth century.

Give yourself some control over FOMO (fear of missing out) on social media. If you see 'friends' out without you and repeated perceived slights like this are messing with your self-esteem, stop all notifications from those friends. Try it: you are worth so much more than a tick in someone's box.

If you don't like something you see, that does not make it a crime. Practise not reacting. If someone who you know to be deliberately provocative says something that seems opposed to everything you stand for, maybe instead of reacting emotionally, go mad by rolling your eyes and tutting. And then move on to something else.

The pottering year

Pottering is a year-round activity but there are points in the calendar when you might lean towards certain types of pottering. This is driven by circumstances, free time and the weather.

Looking out of the window

Looking out of the window while sitting down is especially relaxing if there is something pretty to look at like the trees and flowers of a garden, or the comings and goings of birds on a bird feeder. However, if you have been having a sit down for quite a while – so long in fact that you're feeling a bit fidgety and bored – it's time you moved.

Rise from wherever it is you are sitting and stretch, go to the window, pull the curtain aside, settle your eyes on the middle distance and stare blankly. Stand for a moment. Observe the scene: the bin men, someone walking their dog, a nice car, a flowery front garden.

Catch a hello from a neighbour, smile and wave them over for a chat. Take note of the weather: is it worth popping out while it's fine, or does it look a bit nippy? Are you going to stay in or go out? One way or the other, pottering can make you surprisingly impulsive.

The garden

Being outside accompanied by plants, trees, a breeze and birdsong is just good for you. Tending, nurturing and checking over greenery in balcony pots, kitchen herbs on a counter top or an actual small-holding is the peak of seasonal pottering. It begins in spring with giving the paths a quick sweep and the lawn its first mow. Enthusiastic gardeners may do such things as germinating seeds, followed by pricking out and transferring seedlings from small pots to bigger pots to the ground. For everyone else, simply watching things getting bigger is a satisfaction. Looking over your plants gives you a reason to keep going outside into your garden.

Throughout the growing period in spring, summer and into the autumn, you can take a low-maintenance approach to gardening. The advantage of inexpert gardening is that your plants can thrive despite some benign neglect. Much like us, plants need food, water and sunshine. Stick on some compost. Fill a watering can and swish it to and fro wherever and whenever the soil looks dry. Snip at untidy leaves and twigs with scissors if you don't have proper gardening tools. Do light, regular weeding by pulling up things that shouldn't be there. Dig over bare earth. Run your hands through and over the leaves of fragrant plants like lavender and rosemary. Pick over and deadhead flowers like geraniums to encourage growth. Periodically, you'll need to collect up stray leaves or set straight an upturned garden chair or a spade that has fallen over in a strong wind. When not in use, stack plant pots one inside another, in ascending size order, smallest to largest.

For more detailed advice, go to your local library to borrow a book on gardening. Take a bus to your local garden centre and browse what's blooming and pretty. Or, even better, get chatting to neighbours who have gardens that look impressive and appear to indicate that the owner actually knows what they're doing. Borrow (and return) implements from expert gardeners of your acquaintance. Seek advice from them.

Birds and wildlife

Somehow, watching another species being busy is restful: bees visiting flowers, a dragonfly over a pond or the comings and goings of birds in your surroundings. Having a bird feeder keeps you looking out of the window. Fill it up once a week; and occasionally, when the feeder is empty, give it a good wash with warm soapy water to keep the feeder clean and the birds healthy. And then sit in your garden and watch nature's endeavours to get on.

—

Leisure time in the garden
Frisbee, shooting hoops and keepie-uppies are all activities that you don't have to do for too long, spend too much time doing or put too much effort into.

Buy cards and presents
Find out when people's birthdays are and make a note of the dates on your calendar. That way you can send people a card in plenty of time and you will gain a reputation for 'being good at birthdays'. Acquire cards for all occasions when you are out and about so that you can dip into a ready stack in a timely manner.

Find presents when you're on holiday or going out for the day, and from specialist shops in your local area. If you see the perfect gift for someone, buy it there and then, especially if they are really good at buying you presents and you would like to return the favour.

Make social arrangements
Phone people and invite them to join you for a quick coffee, an evening cinema trip or an entire day out.

Or set a date for friends to come round. Every so often invite someone new to widen your social circle; ask a friend to bring a friend. Propose a selection of dates.

On the appointed day, make something nice to eat. Cooking is one of the great pottering activities. Peruse some good recipes, wander down to the shops to find the ingredients and follow this with chopping, prepping and assembling. The food doesn't have to be gourmet. The easier the better (roast in winter, barbecue in summer, pasta at other times of the year). It's the good company that counts. Make it a digital-free occasion.

Ideally, your guest will invite you back to their place. If you have accepted an invitation, stick to that arrangement. On no account should you accept a better offer. If you have previous commitments, turn down invitations gracefully and suggest another date you can get together.

The home-made spa day

You don't have to drive to a former stately home in the countryside to enjoy a spa day. You don't even need to leave your house. Have a bath and a good wash. Find and apply a face pack (you can even make do with what you've got and make your own). Apply a hair treatment. Then smother yourself in something sweet-smelling that's in the bathroom cabinet and that you haven't got round to using yet.

Put on your dressing gown. Do yourself a mani-cure and pedicure. Make a smoothie with whatever fruit you have to hand, or pour yourself a juice. Semi-recline somewhere comfortable and flick through magazines.

Attend to a pet if you have one

A pet is often good company. Some of them are undemanding. Feed it and chat to it. Clean its bowl and bedding. Stroke it, look into its eyes and take it for a walk (this works for dogs but not so well if your pet is a goldfish). Borrow a dog if you don't have one of your own. You'll come across a whole new realm of people as you wander around your local area with your borrowed pet, and you'll come to excel at small talk.

Spring
Go outside

Find every reason you can to go outside. Go into your garden and sit on a chair. This doesn't have to be a special garden chair; you can drag one out from your kitchen.

—

The great clothes migration (spring)

When the weather begins to warm up, put away your cold-weather clothes and coats, gloves and hats and get out your clothes for warmer weather, like T-shirts and shorts.

Spring cleaning

Is it the change in the temperature and weather that triggers a fairly major annual cleaning and sorting period? Does the extra light make things look more dusty than they did before? There's no need to begin a cleaning frenzy; just go and sort out a single cupboard. Sometimes that is enough.

–

Summer
Going on holiday

The most relaxing holidays are those where you don't do or plan very much. There's no rush to do anything or be anywhere. You potter into town to look around the local shops and market and perhaps pick up a few bits to assemble into a lunch (cheese, fruit, bread). You sit in a cafe having a coffee, a look about and a good think. Then you make your way back to your accommodation slowly. After lunch, you sit again and read your book, the afternoon stretching before you. Eventually the evening arrives and you potter into town again.

There is no need to have researched a restaurant in advance. When you start to feel a bit hungry, look out for a nice cafe or restaurant – and go in to see if they have a table. If they haven't, ask them for a local recommendation, or enquire when it might be less busy. When you sit at a table ask for a menu to peruse, even if you already know what you're going to have. Throughout the holiday look at your surroundings –

you're by a pool or in a pretty town – or as you wander on a beach, collect pebbles and shells. Put a few in your pocket and throw the rest back in the sea. Write your name in the sand and arrange seaweed and stones into an approximation of a mermaid with wild hair.

–

Make ice and ice lollies
Fill an ice-cube tray with water. Make your own ice lollies with fruit juice.

–

Go fruit picking
Head into the countryside and stop by the first fruit-picking farm you come to. Take along containers to fill with strawberries and raspberries. When you come home and realize you have more fruit than you can ever eat, make jam.

–

Give your houseplants some attention
When the light is brighter, the dust that has settled on the leaves of houseplants is more noticeable. Give each of the leaves a quick wipe and trim off any dead bits. Don't forget to water your houseplants throughout the year. They will need less water as the weather gets cooler. When you notice that a plant has got too big, rummage in the shed or garden for a new container. You may derive satisfaction from filling the pot with soil from the garden, because you haven't got any compost, and finding the right-sized saucer to go underneath.

Autumn
Start a course

Courses begin throughout the year, but the back-to-school month of September feels like the right time to start learning something new. Whether it's for a ballroom dancing taster session, a public lecture on astrophysics or a six-week course on bicycle mechanics, buying new stationery will get you in the right frame of mind and make it feel official. Finding out how to do something – like learning to play the guitar or speak a new language, or a practical skill like woodworking – will leave you with an enormous sense of achievement.

–

Plant bulbs

The right moment to plant bulbs is when you find yourself kicking through leaves on the ground (swish! swish!). Planting bulbs is very easy: buy some bulbs, fill a pot with compost or dig a hole in the ground, put the bulbs in, cover with earth. The flowers will wake up as spring arrives.

–

Do yourself a future favour

It's a mucky job, but give your barbecue a thorough clean before you retire it for the winter. Put it away somewhere dry so it doesn't get rusty. Think how pleased you'll be when the warm weather arrives and the grill is without the previous year's grease and ashes.

The duvet
Every few months, go to the launderette to wash your duvet. Sit in the warmth, smell the wet-soapy air and listen to the rumble of the dryers.

–

The great clothes migration (autumn)
When it begins to get cold, put away your T-shirts and shorts and get out your colder-weather clothes and coats, gloves and hats.

–

Wrap presents for Christmas and write cards
Buy presents throughout the year and then wrap them well ahead of Christmas. Write Christmas cards too.

Winter
Christmas
You'll be away from work and the days stretch before you. You've got food in, so you won't need to go out. Make the most of leftovers and don't forget to move about once in a while.

–

Make marmalade
It's a faff – as making marmalade takes hours – but that very fact gives you a good excuse to stay at home all day. And by the end your house will smell amazing.

Snuggle

Avoid bitter winds and frost by staying in and tucking yourself up under a blanket. Cosy. Read a book, look out of the window or phone a friend.

—

Plan how the rest of the year will go

The new year comes very quickly after Christmas and you may find you make resolutions in a rush. Try giving yourself a few extra days to ponder what's most important to you and what you could try to do over the next year. If you're still off work, potter and save 6 January, Epiphany, to make plans and decisions about the coming months.

8

'Planning' and achievement

Time spent pottering is uncharted territory. Though you may not know the specifics in advance, if you want to do it for any length of time it is prudent to put aside some time.

Marking out this terrain often begins with a declaration of intent. When someone asks you what you're doing at the weekend, for example, you say, 'Oh, I don't know really. Just pottering.' What this really means is that you haven't decided yet, you don't want to commit to anything, and you could perhaps do with a bit of time on your own. Being non-committal like this puts you in control because you actually have a plan – to do not very much. If, however, they follow up their query with an exciting invitation, feel free to abandon all plans to potter and join them. Remember that pottering is infinitely flexible and so you can potter another time.

However, should you wish to proceed with your pottering plans, perhaps pottering for a whole day, you will want to make the most of it. Plan ahead and do essential activities like paying bills or doing a Big Shop at a supermarket beforehand. Serious activities such as filling in a mortgage application also don't belong in pottering days, nor does being on your computer or phone sorting out utilities and financial admin. So get important, boring and necessary things done. Use velocity to get things out of the way with the aim of slowing right down and having 'a nice sit down' later.

You can 'plan' for pottering in several ways:

Make pottering part of your usual routine: get up in the morning and set the kitchen straight before you leave the house. This is so unconscious that you may well not know you are doing it.

—

Set aside a regular time for pottering. At the weekend, say, or an evening when you have to be in. This is a time you 'like to be free'; but what you really mean is that you are free to do whatever you want at home, i.e. you are not really available at all.

—

Keep a date in mind when you plan a day for pottering to go 'into town'. Book a day off work or from your usual responsibilities. Do this with enjoyment and without guilt. Try not to let anyone hijack your time with a question that begins 'Could you just …?' No, you couldn't.

—

Go on holiday with no plans to do anything. You know that when you get there, you'll be occupied one way or another. Book accommodation and a means to get there. When you arrive, go with the flow.

Micro-pottering

You can do pottering anywhere. Pottering can take as much time as you need and as much time as you have. It is something that you can pick up and drop at will. This is especially true of micro-pottering: those moments in the day when you do something that is not strictly necessary but gives you a short break, like washing the goo off a soap dish. You may need only a few moments out of your day to readjust your thoughts, and you can do it wherever you are and without realizing it. You might find yourself making papers at work less messy by banging the pile on your desk along one edge, then doing a quarter turn and banging again. Done. It's as if a small restoration of physical orderliness – such as lining up sticky notes into a neat stack or sharpening pencils – helps bring about a tidy mind. Micro-pottering is almost always spontaneous.

The benefits of having a think

Pottering activities such as looking out of a window and having a think achieve more than you realize. They let you clear your mind and explore your thoughts. Ponder the big questions: what makes me happy? Should I move house/jobs/direction? Stop to think about the good things in your life and list them in your mind. Literally count your blessings.

You don't have to come up with definitive answers, but this could be an unintended consequence. Having a think is all about the process, not the results.

Think about the simpler things: what shall I eat later; what shall I do at the weekend; can I get away with wearing my comfiest clothes out in public – is anyone really going to notice if I wear a big coat over the top? Then, of course you can engage in the best kind of thinking: daydreaming. Wishful speculation allows you to go from pleasant thought to pleasant thought, revisiting familiar, well-worn positive scenarios. They never actually have to happen. What would you do if you won the lottery? Speculate about how you would spend all that money. Think about which celebrity would be your friend if you had gone to school with them before they were famous. Contemplate your contingency job (that is, one that you're not doing now but that looks exciting and interesting in theory – one that you would do if salary, ability, training and practicalities were no object, like basketball player or sheep farmer).

Pottering when you really need it

It is worth acknowledging that there are times in life when it can feel as though you are constantly occupied with doing and thinking about other people's priorities and expectations: work and family and stress and studying. When you recognize that your time is not your own, you can gently nudge yourself back into control of some tiny aspects of your life. No one can stop you from making beans on toast or walloping the doormat on the front step.

You might find yourself using pottering in the gravest of circumstances as a distraction technique: at a hospital bedside, at the wake after a funeral, after a break-up. It's as if you want to counterbalance the gravity, distract yourself and give yourself a moment to escape.

With pottering you never have to be perfect. There are no targets, you don't have to achieve anything and you can retreat into a private sphere. It allows for flexibility, and because there's no need for perfection, there's no pressure. That means that during times of difficult circumstances – when you have so much else to do – pottering is a chance to have a moment free of responsibility. If pottering were to belong to the positive psychology family, it would be a kind and benign aunt. It doesn't take much to impress her: she is gentle, she smiles a lot and she says, 'Don't be so hard on yourself. You should be really proud, the way you handled that.'

On occasion, pottering can offer a coping strategy. It is, though, just one thing in an armoury of self-care. Pottering offers no promises about making you more resilient. It won't solve your problems, but it might give you a temporary rest, so that you can gather your resources and strength to tackle the things that matter.

Pottering, not procrastination

Are you mentally pacing around a thought, problem or task? Are you putting something off until the last minute? Are you looking for a distraction? Are you seeking out diversionary activities?

Pottering can help you work through your thoughts, but make sure you are pottering, not procrastinating. Pottering is most often a temporary activity because – eventually – real life gets in the way. Pottering allows you to clear your mind, and that mental decluttering can give you a chance to re-evaluate your life, for your thoughts to come together. Once your pottering is done and over, you can get on with the business of working, sorting out your life and doing the things that need to be done.

Pottering is guilt-free. If you have been occupied for a while to avoid doing something necessary and you are beginning to feel guilty, you are procrastinating, not pottering.

Dealing with procrastination

Realistically, you do have to get on with your life. Pottering is not an entirely full-time occupation, because that would not be realistic, possible or affordable. Unless, of course, you are a millionaire who likes nothing better than tinkering with something in your shed or flicking through your collection of rare first editions. And you have staff to do everything else for you.

Is there a point when you feel a nagging sensation that you should be doing something else and that feeling becomes more persistent? Use these strategies to get it done. You can come back to pottering another time:

Recognize that you are procrastinating.

–

Decide that you should probably stop pottering and do something constructive.

–

Look closely at the reasons for your procrastination. What is it that you are trying to escape, and why are you trying to escape it? Are your reasons reasonable?

–

Is perfection getting in the way? Give yourself a gentle talking to and say to yourself, 'Done is better than perfect.'

–

Prioritize. Write a list of the things you have to do in the order you have to do them. A list can give you focus and a sense of purpose.

Decide upon a firm deadline for stopping pottering (e.g. after finishing something or at a specific time).

—

Remove yourself from distractions. For the potterer, this means being well away from the kitchen, the garden and large cupboards.

—

Start one of the items on your list, work at it, and when you're finished reward yourself with a micro-potter, doing one small thing like pulling the wilted blooms from a flower arrangement. Then turn to the next thing on your list.

—

You can have a longer potter when everything on the list is done.

Commonsensefulness

Commonsensefulness (a combination of common sense and mindfulness) is thinking about what's good for you – and then acting on it. Obvious, really.

Spend time with people you like.

—

Do the things you love.

—

Take people up on invitations and send them out in return.

Be kind.

–

Appreciate the small things.

–

Take a moment to celebrate your successes.

Common sense comes with life experience, observation and reflection. In fact, pottering is all common sense. Think of the five basic rules:

Make do with what you've got (exercise your practical expertise with everything from making a dinner out of leftovers to polishing your shoes).

–

Don't try too hard (especially if you are feeling a bit overwhelmed and you need to take it easy).

–

Movement (that's just sensible).

–

Keep it local (pottering gives you a sense of community).

–

Keep it digital-free (it's for the best).

Achievement

Some might consider that a day spent pottering is a day 'doing nothing' and is a 'waste'. However, for something that relies so heavily on self-restraint, moderation and temperance, you can achieve a surprising amount while pottering: sorting out, cooking, attending to the garden, doing hobbies and DIY. Pottering can also give you a change in atmosphere, pace and location. It offers the chance for mental rumination, decluttering and tidiness, without pressure or judgement. It also gets you out of the house, into your community and talking to your neighbours.

Each individual pottering principle can help you feel content – and in combination the effect is exponential. There is nothing more valuable than that.

Epilogue:
Will pottering really change your life?

Is pottering going to change your life? I honestly can't guarantee it.

However, what I like about it so much is that pottering allows you to have control over your own circumstances, letting you become free from the tyranny of demands on your time. When I was at my absolute busiest, I would get up really early and make dinner to come back to that evening. Usefully, social media provides reminders. Here's a post from that era:

'Another one of those mornings. Flung together roast red pepper and filo parcels to pop into the oven later. Put the laundry on. Comforted someone crying about actual spilt milk (the whole bottle). Picked up glass and mopped floor. Dried someone's pants. Made sandwiches. Did ponytails. Got to school for ten past eight.'

Ten past eight? How on earth did I manage to do that? Why didn't someone make me sit down? That post wasn't about being a 'super-mum'. That post was about a woman who needs a rest from the daily chaos and using ten minutes she didn't really have to make something nice to eat and look forward to at the end of the day.

Here's another:

'Yesterday was one of those days. Internet shop was 45 minutes late so had to unpack the lot in the two minutes before we left for school, shouting about cardigans and shoes. And then work was fine. And then after school I walked five children back in the rain, and acquired another four children. Two people came round to give me quotes to sand the floor. Five of the children left, I got two of the remaining children to Guides and then I acquired another child for a sleepover. How many children is that?'

I'm still not sure. Did I end up with more children than I started with? I don't think any went missing. My children have never even been to Guides, so who was I taking? This shows the mental agility required to navigate parenthood and remember stuff not just for yourself but for innumerable other people too.

Social media is useful for reminding you about things you had forgotten, but some things you don't

forget. I never used social media to post anything about looking after my dad, who was ill at the same time as the usual parenting chaos above (and the full-time job on the other side of London). But I do remember going to A&E quite a lot, sitting and watching TV with him, hospital appointments and, on one occasion, him being in hospital at the same time as one of my children (so that was handy). Actually, that might have happened more than once; it's a blur, if I'm honest. I don't regret a single minute of that period of my life: I was pleased to have spent so much time with him.

When you come out of a period of grief, preceded by a period of caring, not surprisingly you are a bit socially inept, because those two situations are lonely and you're cut off from people. In my case I over-compensated for the isolation by being an utter doormat. I did things for people that were a massive effort for me, and they just didn't notice. I said it was no prob-lem at all that people cancelled at short notice or were several hours late, that I hosted large social occasions but didn't receive invitations in return.

Luckily, I realized eventually that this approach did me no good whatsoever, so I stopped trying so hard. Around that time I was also overly optimistic about my employment prospects. I was frequently cross about not getting one of the jobs I applied for. I realize now, of course, that though I had plenty of good experience and was capable, I probably didn't come across as having the required energy and 'hunger', because I was a bit tired with everything. One time, I applied for a role that I thought I would be good at, and I didn't even get an interview. That triggered a 'bloody well sod it, why am I even bothering' moment, and I booked off several Tuesdays in a row.

Tuesdays? Why Tuesday? It's not the most popular day of the week. This is a plus if you're attempting to persuade a manager that you're not going to be in for one day each week, because it doesn't clash with other people's one-day holiday requests (usually on a Monday or Friday). It's often free of significant meetings, so I wouldn't be missing anything major. And it's the day of the week when I worked a short day (between ten and two, for school pick-up and drop-off), which meant I could use half a day's leave, but have *an entire day all to myself.*

I lent a sheen of legitimacy to this part-time career break by 'having some plans'. I was going to do two things: clear the loft and build a very small brick wall around the flowerbeds in my garden. To this day I have done neither of those things.

I didn't know it at the time, but those Tuesdays were pottering days. I would get up early to make the most of the day. I did a bit of cooking, rummaging and cleaning of milk bottles. I signed up for an evening course to extend the hours of the day that belonged to me. I travelled to London from the suburb where

I live, looking out of the window or reading a book. When I got into town I wandered about the shops, then did something spontaneous like doing one of those department store free make-up demonstrations or going to a public lecture at a museum.

Most of the time, though, I was at home and in my local area. I couldn't tell you specifically how I spent most of my time. I did hang out with my bewildered and uninterested cat Pippa, and I joined the gym (the nearest one, not a shiny, high-pressure one). I made long-overdue appointments with the dentist, hairdresser, optician and doctor for checks and general maintenance. I made a superficial effort in the garden. I filled up my bird feeder and watched the birds come and go. I might have made jam. I did some sewing because it's my thing, and I went out to get fabric and haberdashery from a market, a shortish bus ride away, during which I looked out of the window some more.

I had cups of tea with lovely people and waved hello to my neighbours. I found all the people I could rely on. I talked on the telephone. I was on social media occasionally and did watch a single box set (a Scandi thriller, which wasn't compatible with sewing because I couldn't read the subtitles outlining the complicated plot and concentrate on my needle and thread at the same time), but other than that I didn't really engage with my digital life on Tuesdays.

So how did pottering change my life even just a little bit? It's not that much of a mystery, really. A woman who has done a bit too much for a bit too long gets completely overwhelmed and gives herself the opportunity to have a rest.

Having some time off to potter allows you to take pleasure in small things. It teaches you to be resourceful, patient and slow. Crucially, your time is your own. I couldn't tell you that I had a lot to show for my Tuesdays, because faffing about having a think doesn't look all that productive, but actually *giving yourself some time and putting effort into yourself* is hugely beneficial, no matter how you choose to do it, and when you allow yourself to opt out of pressure, the answers come to you.

After six Tuesdays off I was more relaxed and had a different perspective. I was ready to redo my CV and lined up a couple of recruitment fairs. I had time to think about what I was really good at and spent some time working out how I could better articulate my expertise. Once I did that, I – seemingly magically – got on an apprenticeship scheme and was promoted. I couldn't have done that had I not been in a good frame of mind, or if I had hurried the application and preparations.

What else did I learn?

Don't try too hard. Rushing makes people think you don't care, and a calm demeanour masking inner turmoil means that people will believe you when you say you're fine. Instead of doing things you 'should' do, notice something you should do and then ignore it. It's incredibly empowering. By taking some time to not strive for your goals, you might end up achieving them anyway.

—

Make do with what you've got. It is environmentally friendly, but it also means making the best of your circumstances as well as the resources you have to hand. It is worth remembering that you can always rely on yourself.

—

Movement. Go and be with people who think you are great. Be in your local community. And do some exercise.

—

Keep it local. You don't need to go anywhere fancy to have a good time. If you are with the right person you can have an excellent time wandering down to the shops to pick up bin bags.

—

Keep it digital-free. Make the most of your day. Once in a while, go and do something interesting, so you have something to talk about and look forward to. It doesn't matter whether it is impressive or trivial: it's better than being held captive by your digital devices.

Everyone has their own way to recharge, and pottering is mine.

Thanks

When I asked my husband, Paul, how he would like to be credited in this book, I had in mind to gush about how wonderful he is. He said, 'Just tell them the only reason you have had time to potter and write is that I did all the vacuuming and ironing.' He's probably right. Thanks babe. For a million things. I love you.

Thanks to him and the other people who were involved in the early conversations and drafts of this book: Tim, Fran, Pádraig, Steve, Adrian, Chris, Stacey, Gemma, Tracy, Chloe, Dom and especially Martin.

Thank you very much Katherine, Monika, Steph, Tamsin, Emma, Pat, Kate and Bethan for your Wednesday-morning interest in 'Big Fun Tuesday'.

And thank you to all the other people who are good to me, especially Dominic, Phoebe and Louisa. Also Jo, Lynsay, Lil, Rita, Pat, Chris, Mabel, Dorothee, Angi, Fiona, Martina, Veronika, Jo, David, Bill, Christina and my lovely Auntie Cathie. Kate who wrote me a letter, Tallulah who invited me along, and Emily who thought we should meet for pizza: thank you for your kindness. A wave and a hello to the Mayfield ladies not already mentioned. Cheers to Terry and Nick, who taught me how to do tiling, and to Jan and Jenna in the deli, and Lee in the butcher's, thanks for the chat.

I wouldn't have known about *l'arte dell'arrangiarsi* without a thorough explanation from Veronica Di

Grigoli, the blogger/author behind *The Dangerously Truthful Diary of a Sicilian Housewife* (www.sicilian-godmother.com). Thanks Veronica!

And finally, thanks to Pippa the cat and Brandie the dog, for being silly and good company.

Who is Anna McGovern?

Anna has been working for the BBC on digital projects since 2001. Ordinarily, when she's not doing that, she lives a busy, no-time-for-scented-candles life surrounded by three children and a distressed cat. A while ago, after applying for a job and not getting an interview, she decided to take off one day a week to potter and recharge. One day a week for six months she did whatever she pleased. Anna found it to be most beneficial.

Charlotte Ager is an illustrator living in London and originally from the Isle of Wight. She loves drawing's ability to be moving and soft, but also utterly silly.